The REAL SECRET Behind the SECRET of TRUE SUCCESS

BRIAN P. LUCAS

Copyright © 2018 by Family Priority Publishing

All rights reserved. No part of this publication may be reproduced, distributed, or transmitted in any form or by any means, including photocopying, recording, or other electronic or mechanical methods, without the prior written permission of the publisher, except in the case of brief quotations embodied in critical reviews and certain other noncommercial uses permitted by copyright law.

Brian P. Lucas is not a CPA, accountant, lawyer, and/or attorney and is in no way, shape, or form legally representing and/or providing you with any legal advice in any capacity. All of the subject matter provided herein is for informational purposes only. Brian P. Lucas does not guarantee you results. You and only you are responsible for what you do or don't do with the information provided, so due diligence on your part is an expected and appreciated requirement.

Family Priority Publishing
P.O. Box 1470
Gibsonton, Florida 33534

ISBN: 978-1-7324104-0-4

10 9 8 7 6 5 4 3 2 1

Printed in the United States of America

Lifetime Thanks

To my wife, Jan G. Lucas, who believes in me, cares for me, and loves me unconditionally, even when I do not know or understand how to believe in, care for, or love myself—a strong woman who has the eyes to foresee the person I am today, discrediting and contradicting the rest of the world, who told me I would be either in prison or dead by the age of 21. She is a caring woman who has loved me for me from the very beginning, not for what she could get from me, because I can assure you that I had nothing beneficial or productive to give when we met.

Jan sacrificed her time and energy to a lost and hopeless child who was full of pain and bitterness toward the world and everything in it because she could see his potential to become a man who had something to offer. She willingly endured the growing pains of a boy as he matured and learned to become the man full of wisdom, knowledge, and power that she always knew was within.

She is an independent and self-sufficient woman who refuses to settle for less or accept mediocrity, no matter the circumstances, with or without the approval of others; a natural-born leader who understands the importance of being quick to hear and slow to speak; a silent but deadly opponent at the snap of a finger; an empowering and encouraging woman who always reminds me to utilize the negatives from my past to create a better future and tells me that the greatest way to silence the doubters and naysayers is simply to succeed.

My wife is a soldier, always hands-on, never sitting on the sidelines, and a true representation of the support any real man needs to stay focused and continue to push forward through each phase of life.

Jan is a Christian who says what she means and means what she says, who loves and trusts God and is a true representation of who and what she believes in, even till her death.

Jan brings light to the dark, smiles to the sad, joy to the brokenhearted, love to the hurt, strength to the weak, and hope to the hopeless; to say she has a strong work ethic, excellent morals, great character, and a magnetic and cheerful attitude that is contagiously motivating would be an understatement.

Jan is the most Christ-like of anyone I have ever encountered in my life, a true woman of God who is full of faith and walks what she talks!

To my wife: Jan, I need you to know that I love you, I miss you, and I am eternally grateful for every investment you made into my life in the last nineteen years that has undisputedly played a major role in making me the man I am today.

I will always love you, Jan, and I will see you again.

Brian P. Lucas

BRIAN P. LUCAS

Dedication

I dedicate this book to each and every one of you who has invested your time and energy into reading this book and is seriously interested in implementing the changes required to be the best you that you desire to be. Congratulations for taking a step forward toward improvement for yourself and your family. I wish you all the very best to truly succeed in all your endeavors, and I encourage you to keep reading books, learning new things, and exposing yourself to experiences that challenge you to make sacrifices and implement changes that ultimately promote growth and development.

Family:

To my mother, Sandra Lucas, who is one of the three most powerful women I have ever encountered in my life and has exemplified the true definition of Agape Love. I am extremely thankful that when I was fifteen (while I was away from home on one of my many childhood vacations), she enlightened me that life is a game, and she encouraged me to quickly master the mindset and attitude to learn how to consistently win the game by having the eyes to see things for what they really are rather than accepting things at face value and falling into the purposeful trap that has been set for me to continue to fail. Although the message did not resonate overnight and change did not come immediately, I am able to look back and reflect on the fragments that contributed to my personal growth and development, and I am forever appreciative of her wisdom. I am likewise thankful to my immediate family, David Hayes, Joshua Hayes, Victoria Hayes, and Lawrence Hayes; Jan G.

Lucas, Wilfred Odom, and the Magee family; Belva Doby and family, with a special thanks to Eric T. Walker for looking out for me and showing me the way of survival at the age of thirteen; and Jeneen D. Alexander for granting me a second chance at life and loving me the best way she knew how. And to my ride or die street family that I am no longer affiliated with, I sincerely thank you for being that family outside the family that implemented a sense of loyalty and living by a code, although, respectfully, we no longer share the same spiritual beliefs.

Personal:

To Lisa M. Marrero, who has sacrificed daily, wholeheartedly, with genuine love, affection, and a sincere concern for my wellbeing, and invested her time, energy, and resources into me and my family without ceasing or complaint, I am beyond appreciative and grateful for everything that you have done for me, and I pray that God will bless you to continue to be a blessing accordingly: F-T-O-T-T-S-3. James Murphy, Lavonsky D. Hawthorne, and Vinson Keyhea, I sincerely appreciate you. Linzi S. Morris is by far the most active, dependable, and reliable member of our network, who has worked tirelessly and gone above and beyond to assist with the completion of this project without reserve; she has made it a point to actively practice and live out what we teach by implementing the basic concepts of this book to encourage herself, her family, and others to live the best lives that they can right now.

I thank Pastor Henry L. Babers, Sr., and First Lady Ernestine Babers for being real and accepting me for who I am without judgment or condemnation and allowing God to use them to be a blessing in my life and instrumental in my next phase of growth and development; Parkview Christian Life Center Family and Ministers for welcoming me with open arms; and

Dedication

Luis Rodriguez for challenging me and seeing past my aggressive and rough demeanor and providing me with the opportunities to build my character and work ethic with a major corporation, which opened up several doors of opportunity (including real estate) that I may have never encountered otherwise. Last but not least, I especially thank the Tampa Bay Area Lennar Team, who were like family to Jan, and all of the professionals, friends, associates, and homeowners for being supportive and showing their love, honor, and appreciation in cherishing her memory.

Table of Contents

A Personal Journey xiii

Foreword xvi

Introduction xvii

Chapter 1: Personal Definition of Perfection 1

Chapter 2: Living by Your Own Definitions 5

Chapter 3: Stop Running the Rat Race 11

Chapter 4: Power of the Three-Letter Word 21

Chapter 5: The Mindset of the Wealthy 27

Chapter 6: Building a Successful Team 33

Chapter 7: The Secret Behind the Secret 41

Appendix 49

Bonus Chapter: More Than Enough 51

The Conclusion 69

About the Author 71

A Personal Journey

Five years ago, I became a single mom with six children. I was working two jobs, and ends still weren't meeting. I was fed up, worn out, burned out, and just plain tired. I had two broken-down cars, one of which was literally pushing up daisies. The other had almost two hundred thousand miles on it and was in constant need of repair. My credit wasn't horrible, but it wasn't great either. I drove fifty miles round-trip to get everyone to school and myself to work each day. I lived in an apartment that I was renting, in a complex I didn't want to live in.

One day, I read a story similar to others I had read over the years. These stories were about young adults who had achieved something great in their lives. They were happy for themselves, but they all wished that their moms could be there to be happy for them. Their moms had literally worked themselves to death trying to make a way for their children. I didn't want that to be me—I want to experience all of my children's successes.

At the time, my primary goal was to have enough money to sustain the life I had then. However, I now know that way of thinking was limited. I had to change the way I thought. While I only thought to rent a better apartment, I now own a house, which at the time I thought was unattainable. I used to want a better job to make more money, but now I am working toward working for myself so that I'm not spending most of my productive hours of the day making someone else money.

I now understand that the money I spend should have a purpose and be an investment in my future, not just a frivolous purchase that will not benefit me in the long run and will keep me in bad debt. I know that I have to control my finances, that improving my credit opens up my access to more credit and therefore allows me to keep more of the money I make. More access to funds means more opportunities and more accomplishments. The more I accomplish, the more confident I am that I can do more.

Staying on the path I was on at that time, all I had to look forward to was the same or worse. However, I was determined. If I didn't get it together, my children wouldn't have the exposure they needed to not repeat a mediocre life. I listened, learned, and applied the information in this book. I didn't know what my Personal Definitions of Perfection would be, but I opened myself up to be exposed to greater things and figured out what I wanted to have, not just what I had been told that I should have.

I first had to recognize that I had a problem and needed help. I couldn't get out of this mess alone. I needed a guide, so the first thing I did was pray. I asked God to guide me to be better and do better. Though I didn't realize it at the time, people came across my path who helped steer me in the direction I am going in today, toward my goals.

Now, I live in a house that I own and drive a nice car, and my credit is greatly improved. My children are having their own successes and discovering their own definitions because they have now been and continue to be exposed to so much more.

All this came as I changed my way of thinking. I no longer limit myself as to what I can accomplish. I don't have to settle for less. I can do anything I set my mind to.

There were also sacrifices I had to make. There are people I had to cut out of my life or spend less time with because they had different goals and aspirations than I did, and some had none at all. The time I spent with them meant less time to work on me.

I learned to not let doubts or what other people say sway me. It doesn't matter if they are friends, family, or co-workers—sometimes it is those who are close to you and feel they know you who can plant seeds of doubt and talk you out of taking the necessary steps in your development. I changed the people in my circle whom I allowed myself to be influenced by, because if I wanted to have a better life, I needed to surround myself with and learn from people who are where I want to be now. I want long-term prosperity, not short-term fun.

I understand this book is not one to read once and then leave on the shelf. I am constantly re-evaluating my goals to make sure that I don't lose focus and to see the progress I've made. It encourages me to keep going and gives me a gauge to determine what I have left to do.

No one tells me that it is going to be easy, so what is my alternative? Various people have said that the definition of insanity is doing the same thing over and over and expecting a different result. I didn't want to be one of the many people I see and hear daily complaining about their situations but not enacting any productive changes to make them better.

As I accomplish each goal I've set, I continue to strive toward the rest of them. I know the principles in this book work. It is very possible to produce tangible results by applying them. No matter where you are in your life, whether you are like I was or you are further down the road toward your goals, these principles can be made to work for you.

I am extremely thankful for the guidance and direction I am receiving from *The Real Secret Behind the Secret of True Success* as I grow and develop into the person I truly desire to be.

Linzi Morris
Network Member, Apollo Beach, FL

Foreword

The Real Secret Behind the Secret of True Success, by Brian P. Lucas, teaches you how to attain your personal goals while maintaining a balanced life. This book teaches readers to hold themselves accountable to their choices as they map out the directions of where they want to go in life and exactly how to get there.

There are many decisions that people must make in life, but many times, there is no one there to guide them in those decisions. In this book, Brian encourages you to change and improve your mentality and mindset and guides you toward reaching the level of success that you desire to achieve.

We all desire true success, but sometimes we end up out of balance because we don't know who we truly are. I believe this is one of many reasons Brian invested his time to write this book and also why I decided to write the book *Where Art Thou?*

I encourage you to take advantage of the knowledge Brian P. Lucas shares in this book, as he explains how you may use your real-life experiences to lead you to a more successful and balanced life.

There are secrets behind the secrets of true success!

True success is having balance and knowing who you truly are.

Henry L. Babers, Sr., Pastor/Author
Parkview Christian Life Center
Haines City, Florida

Introduction

First and foremost, this book is not for sensitive people who are easily offended by their own ignorance and have pre-determined not to make any changes to their lives.

I sincerely and respectfully made a choice to move forward with this book, although I am fully aware that I am, for the majority of readers, talking "at" you versus talking "to" you.

Right now, I am basically introducing this book with a full disclaimer:

This book is not a soothing massage therapy or spa-like experience that is here to stroke your ego and make you feel all good and special inside. It's just not!

The fact of the matter is that some things in this book may be rough, come off as rude and somewhat belittling, make you angry or frustrated, and even be very confrontational.

Now stop for a moment—don't throw the book down just yet!

This may actually be good for you. The secret behind the scenes that motivates the feelings is really simple: Anything you read in this book that ruffles your feathers (so to speak); makes you roll your eyes, smack your lips, or feel uneasy or confrontational; seems a bit offensive, belittling, condescending, or hurtful; or makes you angry is more than likely the very area in your life that you need to address the most. Offense only exists if and when something resonates with you; if it didn't, then there would be zero reason to be offended.

Remember, sometimes the truth hurts; nevertheless, it's still the truth.

Now, if you make the excellent choice to read further, then I am assuming that you have granted me permission to speak into your life. I assure you that I will be 100 percent real with you on all levels; I will be very blunt, holding nothing back and telling it just like it is throughout the duration of the book.

Fair enough?

I strongly encourage you to utilize this time as an investment with the hopes of achieving a huge return, and to do so, you will need to eliminate any distractions and make reading, studying, and comprehending each chapter of this book a priority. The one simple thing you miss, skip, or rush through could be the difference between living a great life in a state of More Than Enough versus living with more of the same, which may not be enough.

I look forward to your success as you take this journey one chapter at a time.

Sincerely and respectfully,

Brian P. Lucas

BRIAN P. LUCAS

Chapter 1
Personal Definition of Perfection

Right now, I want you to stop and take a moment to imagine how your life would be in your own realistic definition of perfection. It sounds a little awkward, I know, but trust and be honest with yourself as you imagine perfection; imagine your image, the way you look, the way you dress; imagine your time spent during the day from the time you wake up till you go back to sleep; imagine your home and your family; imagine your car, your vacations, fulfilling your interests, accomplishing your goals, succeeding in every arena of life; imagine your charity and gratuity and giving back to others...

Whatever you define as perfection, put that in your mind right now.

Now stop and ask yourself this one simple question:

Do I have it right now?

It's a very simple, direct, and right-to-the-point question: Whatever you define as perfection, do you have it right now?

Now for most of you, it didn't take two seconds, and the response was an astounding "No!" which is very direct and honest.

For some of you, it may have been a thought of "Yes," followed by "I have Faith that I do" and/or speaking into existence the perfection that has not yet exposed itself, which I completely respect and understand.

Next, we have those very few for whom it is a right here, right now "Yes," and they are actually living a life that they define as perfect for them; that's awesome, and congrats to you if you have been blessed enough to fulfill your own definition. This is an excellent and very rare place to be.

Now stop for a moment, and let's reflect on the question.

Notice I did not ask you if you feel you are living a life of perfection.

I did not ask you if you were living a life of perfection based on the definition of perfection, and I didn't ask you if you were living a life of perfection based on my definition of perfection.

What did I ask you specifically?

I asked *you* if *you* feel *you* were living a life of perfection based on *your* own honest and realistic definition. Now think about that for a moment, because there must be a reason I keep repeating the same thing, right?

OK, let me help you figure out the secret ingredient in this mixture.

Do *you* feel that *you* are living *your* honest and realistic definition of perfection right now?

It doesn't matter what I think, or what Billy, Bob, Jill, or Jane thinks about you. The only person's feedback that matters is yours. You have to live up to your own predefined expectations to be truly fulfilled. The world and the system within have purposely swayed you from these simple truths because that system deters and distracts you from true growth and maturity.

I don't have to tell you that a lack of knowledge and the failure to utilize the knowledge given are detrimental, because you already know that.

The question is, are you willing to allow yourself to be yet another victim who settles for the status-quo definition of perfection

Personal Definition of Perfection

provided to you by the very system that purposely hinders your growth and development?

Yes, you possibly may have been taught to follow the status quo all your life, but what exactly has that done for you, and how is that currently working out for you and your family?

Don't allow your emotions to keep you stranded on a deserted island when there is an able and ready boat waiting for you to come aboard.

No matter what they may look, sound, smell, taste, or feel like, there are limitless opportunities and untapped possibilities in every direction for those who are actively and willingly searching for them.

A person's current situation, past mistakes and failures, and any other negative thoughts that attempt to creep into one's mind are merely unauthorized excuses that must be immediately labeled as the opposition, or better yet, the *enemy*.

Take this same exact time and energy and invest it into positive thoughts, imagining and focusing on the things that you truly desire; your personal reality will be what you believe to be possible and realistic in your life.

Don't expect a million-dollar reality with a five-hundred-dollar belief system!

Being able to clearly comprehend and fully understand your Personal Definition of Perfection is pertinent to your success.

Think it, visualize it, speak it, and then take the necessary action required to obtain the lifestyle that you actually desire; *do not* settle for the definition of life that is being shoved down your throat by the masses!

The bottom line is, a person who "settles for" *cannot, will not, does not*!

Break free and Live by Your Own Definitions!

ACCOUNTABILITY SUMMARY:

What Is Your Personal Definition of Perfection?

Review the first paragraph of the chapter and start piecing your own puzzle together by acknowledging what your Personal Definition of Perfection is.

There are several simple ways to accomplish this task: putting pen to paper, creating a vision board, placing photos and goals on mirrors or computer screens, or whatever other creative measures you are able to think of. Just take action!

Do You Currently Have Your Personal Definition of Perfection Right Now?

YES: What goals and plans do you currently have in place to both maintain your current state and increase it in your next phase?

NO: What actions are you willing to take to obtain it?

A treasure map does *not* make you rich: A treasure map without the treasure is only the direction; you're not rich until you have actually found it.

Chapter 2
Living by Your Own Definitions

Imagine how this world and your life would be if we all followed our childlike hopes, dreams, and ambitions. Remember the child who was innocent and determined before being tainted and manipulated by perverse thinking and the intentional destruction that keeps most people idle-minded, which basically means they will never be a threat to a secret sect of people who are determined to eliminate and destroy their very hopes at ever succeeding in life?

There is a huge misconception from the majority that you are here to please others, and quite frankly, this couldn't be further from the truth and is yet another trick to keep you distracted from what is truly important for you and your family.

Now, stop for a moment and ask yourself this question: How can I live my life to please others when I am not pleasing to myself?

Let me help you here: You can't!

It's sad, because it's a never-ending Rat Race that ends with no fulfillment or accomplishment and more of the same.

Let me ask you a question, and again, be honest with yourself:

Do you think you will ever be able to live a perfect life based on someone else's definition of perfection?

While you're contemplating that question, let me remind you of the question in Chapter 1, where I'm sure the majority of you reading already answered NO, that you don't live a perfect life based on your own definition of perfection, so how will you ever measure up to someone else's definition of perfection?

And that in itself is the problem: Most people confuse whose definition matters in the first place.

The world has a system in place that continues to destroy you and that childlike innocence each and every day by the promotion of thoughts, ideas, and feelings that are contrary and detrimental to what is most important for you and your family.

One of the most successful and overlooked ways is used daily in marketing and advertising: subliminal messaging. The psychology behind *all* marketing and advertising is to make you want more of what everyone else has, do what everyone else is doing, be how everyone else is being, live currently and up to date with technology and style, blend in with the crowd, and not get left behind; however, these are the very tricks that keep most people unfulfilled, depressed, and, more than anything else, *broke*!

Why? Because instead of letting you live out your own life to fulfill your own definitions, the system in place purposely makes you feel inadequate unless you are living your life to fulfill everyone else's definitions. You really have to stop and ask yourself, whose definition means more to you—is it yours, or is it theirs?

Here is an analogy for you to read carefully:

1. You are the door.
2. You are the hinges that control the door's movement.
3. You are the door's handle.
4. You are the lock on the door's handle.
5. You are the key to lock or unlock the lock that controls the door's handle, which uses the support of the door hinges to open and close the door.

Living by Your Own Definitions

It is ultimately *you* who should determine what you will or won't do, and this should be applied to all areas of your life, both personal and business.

Learning to Live by Your Own Definitions is a crucial step to the Real Secret Behind the Secret of True Success! You will not successfully take control of your life if everything about you is defined by someone else!

If you are able to visualize the Lamborghini, Ferrari, Bentley, Rolls Royce, etc., then don't let someone with Ford, Chevrolet, Dodge, and Nissan vision define you and dictate your livelihood.

Remember, don't expect a million-dollar reality with a five-hundred-dollar belief system, and this same rule applies here as well: Don't settle for someone else's definitions and lackluster vision for you and your life but then expect great success.

Now, take a long hard look at your life from the time you were born till right now, and one thing I am willing to guarantee you has been consistent: *conditioning*!

You have been conditioned, influenced, and manipulated your entire life, whether you want to believe it or not!

Please understand that it is not a mistake that most people do not Live by Their Own Definitions and allow other people to dictate and define their lives for them—you have been trained since the day you were born to fall in line and follow the herd.

Start with your parents or whoever raised you—your family, the babysitters, daycares, pre-schools, elementary schools, middle schools, high schools, colleges, places of employment, church and group functions, and the list goes on and on.

Are you truly who you think you are, or are you who you have been conditioned to be?

A conditioned person is the most convenient for the society we live in because he or she is the easiest to control and enslave spiritually, mentally, physically, emotionally, and yes, financially.

Unfortunately, this is the reality we all face daily. What are you prepared to do about it in your life to make a change?

Once you have taken action and made it a point to clearly understand your Personal Definition of Perfection, you can then make the necessary plans, set the required goals, and start Living by Your Own Definitions.

Take control and Stop Running the Rat Race!

ACCOUNTABILITY SUMMARY:

How to Start Living by Your Own Definitions:

First, you must know your Personal Definition of Perfection (Chapter 1).

Next, review and then list some of the major components of importance to you.

For Example:

- *Be a business owner (be specific in regard to the type of business owner).*
- *Have $300k minimum yearly income.*
- *Have $100k minimum liquid cash in the bank.*
- *Start a family (be specific in regard to how many kids, pets, etc.).*
- *Own a waterfront home (be specific).*
- *Own a Bentley GT Coupe (what color, etc.).*

Stop and take a moment to consider whether any of the things you are doing right now will result in your obtaining the items on your list.

For Example:

The list above includes "be a business owner," but if you are currently working for someone else, you are not currently a business owner, and you are not actively making strides to be a business owner, then you are not *Living by Your Own Definitions, and you are currently allowing someone else to define you.*

Now, the list you have created, which is derived from your Personal Definition of Perfection, will become your Desired Destinations that display exactly what your realistic definition of perfection looks like to you.

Next, you are going to take your Desired Destinations and begin making the necessary adjustments and taking the required actions to start Living by Your Own Definitions.

These necessary adjustments and required actions become the Secret Map that displays the step-by-step directions to reach your Desired Destinations.

For Example:

Desired Destination: The goal is to have $100k minimum liquid cash in the bank.

Secret Map: A necessary adjustment may be to eliminate dining out; let's make that worth $1k a month or $12k a year.

This one decision/direction has moved you $12k closer to the $100k goal/destination.

Chapter 3
Stop Running the Rat Race

Most people (maybe even you) have been Running the Rat Race their entire lives!

It is so easy to get swept into the ongoing Rat Race that it is almost second nature to participate. At times, it may actually make you uncomfortable not to be involved, make you feel like you're not accomplished enough or not getting enough things done, or whatever other feeling of inadequacy that may creep in. However, if it is not in your best interest according to your Personal Definition of Perfection, then it simply should not matter to you.

You are not here to prove anything to anybody but yourself—it is *yourself* whom you must please in order to be sufficient, and it is *you* who must congratulate *you* in order to feel true accomplishment. Obtaining your personal definition of sufficiency and fulfilling your honest definition of accomplishment is more rewarding than the whole world admiring you if you have still not met your Personal Definition of Perfection.

Now, I am in no way stating that you should not take other people's feelings and thoughts into consideration, but I am stating that their feelings and thoughts should not sway you from your realistic and honest definition of anything that dictates who you really are.

This is one of many reasons there are so many problems with relationships, be it with your spouse or significant other, family, friends, neighbors, co-workers, church or group members, etc.

You may not believe this or want to accept it, but did you know that most people spend most of their days attempting to both become and imitate things that are completely outside of who they truly are?

Here is a great example: Think of politics and politicians, church and preachers, the military and soldiers, corporate America and managers, or any familiar situation where you have physically seen with your own eyes and heard with your own ears someone talk or behave completely out of character.

Stop and think about that for a moment, because this is nothing new, and this type of character-shifting behavior happens all day, every day.

It can be quite annoying or even aggravating to witness, but you have to understand that this is not their fault, because people in general have been so brainwashed daily to be mere puppets on a string. Going back to the door analogy in Chapter 2, most people are the door, but the key, the handle, the lock, and the hinges belong to Hollywood, video games, TV, radio, entertainers, their jobs, and any other hindrance and distraction you can think of that manipulates them into being someone that they truly are not.

Right now, some of you may be skeptical and reluctant to take personal responsibility, because some of this fits you to a tee, but the best trick the Devil has is to make you think he doesn't exist, and this holds true with every other detrimental character you hold on to.

If you don't believe you can be brainwashed, then the trick is on you, because you are too naïve to ever figure out that you really are brainwashed.

Needless to say, most people will never know or believe that they are nothing more than a bunch of wannabe followers in a pointless

Rat Race that leads to absolutely nowhere, and by the time they find this out, many have no life left to live, so it means little to nothing anyway because they spent so much time blinded by the tricks and deceit of this manipulative society that we live in.

People have been purposely conditioned to be easily controlled followers of a detrimental system that mainly promotes poverty and lack.

Imagine if 50 percent of the population (just 50 percent) were awakened to the fact that they have been intentionally manipulated by a certain sect of people to keep them as far from the truth as possible so that this sect can maintain control; how do you think that would play out?

Sadly, that will never happen, because that would mean people would have to actually stop right now everything they're accustomed to and then learn something or accept something new, which means taking them out of their comfort zone. The simple secret to this disaster is pure laziness: Most people are too lazy to learn anything new or do anything that isn't comfortable or market-worthy.

However, if the new name-brand shoes, phone, tablet, video game, or whatever other worthless, meaningless product were being released, some of you would stand in line from four a.m. to be the first one with it. How ridiculous is that?

The power of marketing and advertising is to brainwash people to always want the newest thing because everyone else will have it, and they don't want to be left out. Meanwhile, they can't afford to put bread on the table, their credit is no good, and they're barely making it from one check to the next, yet they're with the in crowd in the continuous Rat Race, so it's worth it to them because they're accepted.

Now, if that bothers some of you, let me let you in on a little secret: Those words are probably a huge truthful mirror, and maybe you are bothered by what you see—your very own reflection—because that ignorance resembles you in some shape, form, or fashion. I don't know—only you know the truth.

Speaking of truth, next we can discuss the challenges that come with wanting more truth out of life. And it's simple: Most people don't care to know the truth—they only want to feel good and be accepted, which really means and is based off of what, when the very people you want to be accepted by are just as lost (if not more lost) than you are right now?

If most people were completely honest, they would be able to think back as far as they can and remember the bits and pieces of themselves that they have slowly chopped away over the years.

There was definitely a time (maybe even still now) when you were in your own zone, being and doing you, but then you found out it wasn't what the system considers market-worthy or acceptable or cool among your sphere of influence, so you tucked it away and adjusted yourself and who you really are to appease the masses.

Well, let's really think about this for a moment: Ten, twenty, thirty, forty, fifty-plus years of shoving the *real* you to the back burner and taking on the traits the world tells you are acceptable may just change your behaviors, actions, and perspectives on life a little bit, don't you think?

Now you have actually started a civil war within yourself because the you that is being represented and put on display for the world to see is *not* the *real* you; it is the you that you have created to appease the masses, which was dictated and defined by sources outside yourself!

Seriously, why do we wonder why we are not happy most of the time if we are living a life outside of who we truly are, imprisoned and trapped in a fictitious life defined by others?

Why do we take such personal attachment and give such credibility to what other people think about us and what we do? We have been manipulated into believing that what other people think about us really matters, when in all reality, it doesn't, because with my attitude and personality, if I factored in what other people think of me, I would need to be institutionalized.

Now don't get me wrong; I absolutely care about how my character, ethics, and morals are perceived, but at the end of the day, I can't stress and lose sleep over an opinion from someone who will probably never think positively about me anyway. Thus, I am not losing anything, and neither are you.

How can you successfully obtain your Personal Definition of Perfection and start Living by Your Own Definitions if you don't Stop Running the Rat Race?

We have to be very careful that the Rat Race tendencies don't find their way into our Personal Definition of Perfection, or else the achievement and the accomplishment may exclude the desired perfection because they were dictated and defined by the wrong source in the first place.

It is very easy to lose who you really are after so many years of placing the *real* you in the timeout box of life.

I don't want to give out free excuses for everyone to use as crutches; however, you are systematically destined to lose and to be nothing more than a loser, while they simultaneously provide you with a fictitious appearance of winning and being a winner.

The Real Secret Behind the Secret of True Success

Have you ever worked very hard for something and invested all your time and energy into it exactly like you were taught (conditioned) to ensure it would succeed, only to be let down and watch another of your highly invested contributions fail?

You did everything exactly like you were told from numbers one to ten—crossed the T's and dotted the I's, reviewed and revised—yet the end result: *failure*!

Newsflash: Success comes from failure!

Of course, that may seem ridiculous on the surface, but these are the very things the Rat Race will not teach you and prepare you for in life; they would rather make you feel as if you are succeeding in life for their own benefit than admit that better is indeed available to you and your family.

Bottom line, Stop Running the Rat Race—it is an endless rotation that goes nowhere and produces nothing; just because you are busy doesn't mean that you are necessarily productive or beneficial.

You have been told from a young age to go to school and maintain good grades; go to college and obtain a degree; get a good job and start a career; find a mate and start a family; purchase a home, a car, and maybe a pet; save your money, retire, and then live happily ever after.

Does any of this sound familiar to you?

How exactly will this work out for you? Will all your dreams come true following this generational formula of success?

For the majority, the answer is "No," but let's say the answer is "Yes." Now what?

Is that it? Is that all that life has to offer? Sounds a bit robotic, don't you think?

Stop Running the Rat Race

One of the number-one shows on television is called *The Walking Dead*, which is a great example for those who don't opt to Stop Running the Rat Race!

Unfortunately, you have been tricked, duped, hustled, conned, and lied to all your life from one generation to the next; the system has not been set up to promote your success but rather the imitation thereof to keep you conditioned and blinded to the truth.

Have you ever heard the phrase "The rich get richer and the poor get poorer"? How about the statement that this vicious cycle constantly repeats itself, all at the expense of the middle class?

Would you be surprised to hear studies show that the middle class is the meal ticket or, better said, the sucker that basically pays for everything? What success formula do you think the middle class follows? Are any light bulbs shining yet?

Imagine a hamster in a cage running full speed on that lovely wheel of entertainment; the faster the hamster runs, the faster the wheel spins in a majestic rotation that leads to absolutely *nowhere*!

With all due respect, your dad and mom and their dads and moms or whoever raised you do *not* know everything and more than likely grew up under this same exact method of the Rat Race; you really cannot seriously depend on the world, government, teachers, family, friends, neighbors, church, or anyone else, for that matter, to define your Personal Definition of Perfection or to dictate to you how to begin Living by Your Own Definitions.

Sadly, some people will read or hear this, but it won't make it all the way from the first ear to the other—no one really wants to admit to being brainwashed, hustled, conned, tricked, or taken advantage of, mainly because it shows vulnerability, weakness, ignorance, and the need for correction or, best said, change!

I had a conversation with my wife in which she said something that is just so profound to me: "You owe it to yourself to forget everything that you have learned and been taught growing up and begin to seek the truth for yourself."

You have to understand that the Rat Race is banking on you to fall in line, follow the herd, accept the status quo, believe what you are being told without any further investigation or due diligence, and basically play the hand that you have been dealt with no push back.

One way to plan and prepare yourself to understand these challenges is to **discover the Power of the Three-Letter Word!**

ACCOUNTABILITY SUMMARY:

The Accountability Summaries for Chapters 1 and 2 must be completed before attempting to complete this summary.

How to Acknowledge a Potential Rat Race in Your Life:

Anything that distracts you from your goals, contradicts your agenda, compromises your success, or steers you in the opposite direction of your Personal Definition of Perfection is more than likely a contributing factor to the Rat Race.

Review your Personal Definition of Perfection list, vision board, photos, or whatever creative means you decided to utilize, and then simply compare the criteria in question to those of your personal goals and desires that truly define you.

For Example:

If you have ten items listed that represent your Personal Definition of Perfection, and let's say eight items of the criteria in question are opposing those ten items, then that may very well be a Rat Race in your life because it is in opposition to 80 percent of who you feel you are and what you desire.

How to Avoid Becoming a Victim of a Rat Race:

Living by Your Own Definitions is no longer an option—you have to make a conscious effort to make it a mandatory requirement in your life. If you are consistent and persistent with Living by Your Own Definitions, you will immediately acknowledge anything that does not coincide with them and be prepared to avoid it accordingly.

Notes:

Chapter 4
Power of the Three-Letter Word

There is a Three-Letter Word that digs a little deeper and brings out the real motivation behind the scenes for any specific action.

Learning how and when to utilize the Power of the Three-Letter Word may make a huge impact in the effectiveness of your correspondence and communication.

This Three-Letter Word infinitely searches and does not and will not allow a "yes" or "no" answer while thoroughly searching out the truth of any "I don't know" answers; on most occasions, this word is an excellent tool that analyzes everything to get to the root of the problem, situation, or challenge.

This one word enables you to dissect the real reasons that people do the things they do and is so powerful that it has actually become one of my secret words of choice. Strangely enough, it has helped me to build wealth and obtain success, and it may do the same or even more to help you.

The Power of the Three-Letter Word refers to the word *why*.

The power of *why* enables accuracy by describing the what, explaining the when, leading you to the where, and even assisting you with dictating and coordinating a successful how.

Frankly, if you don't know the *why*, then you really don't know much at all that will be productive or beneficial.

Save yourself a lot of wasted time, energy, and money and become vested in the one word that will make an absolute difference in your life.

For Example: Bob wants to buy a phone.

1. *Bob tells you that he wants to buy a specific phone.*
2. *You ask Bob why he wants this particular phone.*
3. *Bob states that it is because he likes the phone.*
4. *Now you ask Bob why he likes the phone.*
5. *Bob answers that he just likes the phone.*
6. *You are now explaining to Bob that you understand that he likes the phone, but the question still remains, why does Bob like the phone? So again, you ask Bob why he likes the phone.*
7. *Bob finally answers the question: "I think the phone is nice."*
8. *Now you ask Bob, "Why do you think the phone is nice?"*
9. *Bob tells you that he likes the way the phone looks.*
10. *You ask Bob why he likes the way the phone looks.*
11. *And then Bob finally answers the very first question you asked him, stating that the reason he wants the phone is that he saw so-and-so with the phone in a music video.*

We don't really need to go any further. See how powerful the word *why* is? So what did we just learn? Bob wants to buy this phone not because he really likes it, not because it's really nice, and not because of the way it looks, but because he saw someone else with the same phone in a music video.

This is what we call Running the Rat Race and playing follow the leader, and you may think this is innocent because it's just a phone, but this is your way of life.

So, is this a purchase that I am willing to make, though it is clearly not a necessity? The answer is "No!" Today it's a phone, then it's shoes, pants, a shirt, hair, makeup, video games, TVs, cars, houses, boats, or whatever else.

Now let's stop for a moment. I'm not stating that Bob doesn't like these things or need these things, but the *why* behind liking them should be able to strongly support buying them.

This works on all categories of conversation, and it may really surprise you once you start figuring out the *why*; you will be amazed how this little yet significant Three-Letter Word can really change your life and your way of thinking and processing information.

Maybe you have heard or read in self-development groups or seminars to "find your why" or something similar, or maybe you have heard or read in management or sales groups or seminars to "find the customer's why" to generate more sales or revenue.

Everyone and everything has a *why*. Whether you can tap into it and understand it or not, the *why* is always there.

For Example:

1. *Any truly successful people will tell you that they listen more than they speak.*
   Why?
2. *Silence is one of the main contributing factors to great negotiations.*
   Why?
3. *You will not figure out the other's why if you are doing all the talking.*
   Why?
4. *If you are doing all the talking, then you are doing little to no listening.*
   Why?

5. You are talking about what you want rather than listening to their why.
   Why?
6. You don't understand the Power of the Three-Letter Word!
   Why?
7. Review numbers 3, 4, and 5 above.

Notice in the example above that number 2 is the initial answer, and numbers 3 through 5 are the *why* (explanations or supporting answers) that aligns with the initial answer.

In addition, numbers 3 through 5 are somewhat repetitive with slightly different delivery, but in the repetition, you can begin to get a feel for when you have successfully executed and exhausted the *why*.

You want to be very careful to utilize the Power of the Three-Letter Word to your benefit, not to your detriment; don't use it to be cocky, condescending, or rude, to show off, or, for the lack of a better word, to be a jerk! *Why* is infinite, but unfortunately, so is ignorance!

Learn how to change your thinking.

ACCOUNTABILITY SUMMARY:

The Accountability Summaries for Chapters 1, 2, and 3 must be completed prior to attempting to complete this summary.

How to Maximize the Power of the Three-Letter Word:

The best way to start is by addressing what will be productive and beneficial for you and your family by finding, learning, and fully understanding your personal *why*.

Upon completion of the Accountability Summary for Chapter 1, you know what your Personal Definition of Perfection is, and upon completion of the Accountability Summary for Chapter 2, you know your Desired Destinations; however, just knowing is *not* enough—you must fully understand the *why*.

Use the PERCS tool below to find out your personal *why*:

Purpose:
Explanation:
Reason:
Cause:
Solution:

For Example:

Desired Destination: The goal is to have $100k minimum liquid cash in the bank.

Purpose: *Why—What is the purpose? To start a business.*

Explanation: *Why—Explain the purpose: To stop working for others.*

Reason: *Why—What is the reason? To stop trading time for money.*

Cause: *Why—Explain the reason: Working for others is trading time for money.*

Solution: *I do not want to work for others, and I no longer want to trade my time for money; $100k will provide me the opportunity to start my own business and assist me with reaching this goal and my Desired Destination.*

Master the Power of the Three-Letter Word:

Practice getting the most *why* out of every conversational opportunity that presents itself each and every day.

Do not settle for mediocre communication and correspondence, and do not leave the conversation without a full understanding of the *why*.

The more time and effort you invest into mastering the Power of the Three-Letter Word, the more rewards, benefits, and opportunities for success await.

Chapter 5
The Mindset of the Wealthy

Now, there is clearly a difference between the way a wealthy person thinks and the way a person who is not wealthy thinks, and it is just naïve or ignorant to overlook the importance of one's mindset.

There was a time in my life several years ago when I had the audacity to make up a bunch of illegitimate reasons that those who are wealthy are wealthy while providing myself with a bunch of unjustifiable excuses for why most are not wealthy.

Now that I am of age and have placed myself in a different environment than I was in when I thought this way and have changed my Circle of Influence and the people I invest my time into, I have had the opportunity to understand that illegitimate reasoning and unjustifiable excuse-making are traits that develop a mindset of those who are *not* wealthy!

What I have come to realize is that if you *think* poor, then you will visualize poor, speak poor, and act poor; the more you think, visualize, speak, and act poor, the more you will *believe* you are poor, which ultimately develops your *mindset*.

A poor mindset prevents a wealthy lifestyle!

Unlike myself years ago, wealthy people don't sit around making excuses for their personal inadequacies to justify their current lack of wealth; they invest their time, energy, and focus on themselves rather than the current circumstances or what things may look like at face value while simultaneously thinking, visualizing, speaking, and acting on the very things that they truly desire, strongly believing they will manifest.

A person cannot sit around thinking poor but expect to be living wealthy!

I was reviewing some articles a few years back, and I came across one that stated that 1 percent of the world's population has more wealth than the remaining 99 percent, and needless to say, this was rather numerically shocking to me; as I continued to read, the article also stated that 1 percent of the world's population owns 95 percent of the wealth, and the remaining 99 percent owns only 5 percent of the wealth.

Did you read what I just wrote?

This article is basically telling me in so many words that 1 percent of people own 95 percent of the wealth, and the remaining 99 percent own the 5 percent of leftovers!

This was a huge eye-opener and game-changer for me personally; if you are able to review these numbers without it sparking something inside of you, then it is very unlikely that you will be making any beneficial changes financially.

Please be advised: I read this article years ago, so these statistics I'm sure have changed since, though I am equally sure it is *not* by very much.

I happen to be extremely analytical, which means I analyze everything to get to the root or, better said, the truth; there must definitely be a valid reason that 1 percent of the world's population has more wealth than the remaining 99 percent.

What is the reason?

One small secret behind why 1 percent of the world's population has more wealth than the remaining 99 percent is that they *do not* do what they manipulate the other 99 percent to do.

What is that exactly?

The 1 percent of the world's population who own 95 percent of the world's wealth *do not* waste their time and money on the very things that they use to generate money from the remaining 99 percent.

Let me write that again: One small secret behind why 1 percent of the world's population has more wealth than the remaining 99 percent is that they *do not* do what they manipulate the other 99 percent to do, which is waste their time and their money on the very things that they use to generate money from the remaining 99 percent.

Again, if you are able to review this information without it sparking something inside of you, then it is very unlikely that you will be making any beneficial changes financially.

Keep in mind, our country recently experienced one of the worst depressions in American history; our fellow American families were losing their jobs and homes, their 401ks and retirement accounts were depleted, the real estate bubble burst, and the economy and the market as a whole basically tanked and hit rock bottom. People were filing bankruptcy, in foreclosure, seeking unemployment. Some, sad to say, were committing suicide, having heart attacks, and panicking due to stress, and the horror stories go on and on. But I want you to stop right now and seriously and sincerely think about those who were *not* affected financially and basically didn't miss a beat during one of our country's worst times in history.

People were struggling in every way imaginable and at their very worst, but when you heard the report of the return on the new movie that just came out, when you saw the stadiums packed to capacity for whatever sports program, when you heard the results for the new phone, video game, or whatever other technology came out, it was as if nothing had ever happened and there was no change!

If that is not an eye-opener to the mindset of the majority, then I don't know what is! People were starving, broke, unemployed, committing suicide, losing their jobs and their homes, in bankruptcy and foreclosure, collecting unemployment and food stamps for the first time, losing their 401k and retirement accounts, and yet for Hollywood, sports entertainment, and many more that I won't name, it was business as usual, earning the same profits if not more, with the same, if not a better, turnout.

So, what exactly am I saying? You, me, we (the remaining 99 percent) are 100 percent of the reason that 1 percent of the world's population has more wealth than the remaining 99 percent, and we are also the reason 99 percent of the world's population owns only 5 percent of the world's wealth: because we do not live day to day as *investors*, and we do not treat everything that we do as an *investment*.

Our waste is their wealth!

Let me write that again: *Our waste is their wealth!*

Really, sincerely think about that.

The Mindset of the Wealthy is that of an investor who strategically invests his or her time into finding new concepts to obtain funds and resources from the consumer; however, the typical consumer usually has no strategy other than to spend and save or save and spend, and neither will provide wealth or a wealthy mindset.

The Mindset of the Wealthy

The consumer's waste is the investor's wealth, and the consumer's lack of knowledge is the investor's key and guarantee of continuous wealth; the less you know and, even more so, do, the less of a threat you are or ever will be.

You have heard the statement "Knowledge is power," but I disagree, because although the book on the shelf is full of instruction, that instruction means little to nothing if you don't pick up the book, read it, and put it to use. Knowledge successfully *utilized* is power, and without utilization, knowledge is nothing more than the unread book on the shelf.

The way you choose to *think* is vital to your success, and it will ultimately determine who you really are and what you truly stand for while simultaneously developing and manifesting your *mindset*.

Implement and utilize the three supporting factors for success!

ACCOUNTABILITY SUMMARY:

The Accountability Summary for Chapter 4 must be completed prior to attempting to complete this summary.

How to Develop the Mindset of the Wealthy:

Starting right now, today, you must make it a point to shift the way you think, visualize, speak, and act to align with the ways that resonate with what you desire for yourself and your family.

Unfortunately, it seems we have been brainwashed into believing that speaking about the things we don't want and speaking against the very things we actually do want will somehow bring about a successful result; this is just not true, nor will it ever be.

Upon completion of the Accountability Summary for Chapter 4, you used the PERCS tool to define your personal *why*, and now you must implement the Mindset of the Wealthy to assist and further enhance your personal development and growth.

Review your PERCS and align your thinking, visualizing, speaking, and actions to support what you desire for yourself and your family.

Chapter 6
Building a Successful Team

Here lies another secret problem among so many that is a contributing factor to burning out, feeling overwhelmed, and, ultimately, failure: People who are consistently trying to do everything on their own will find it very difficult to succeed and overcome every obstacle that stands in their way.

Sadly, even if people do not want to do it on their own, there are so many other people trying to do their own thing too that nothing ever gets done by anyone.

Now, how many people can relate to this?

Right now, I want you to imagine ten people, all on the same page with the same goals, willing and ready to make it happen with a systematic approach to obtain success and to assist you with what you need to accomplish in order to reach your Personal Definition of Perfection.

That would be nothing short of awesome!

I don't care who you are or what you may think. That's a great team!

Why do you think people from other countries come to the United States and are so successful? They come with a team spirit with the same goal; they don't come in a group of ten and have one start a restaurant, one start a car wash, and another start a laundromat. No—all ten of them start the restaurant or nail salon, and they work day in and day out to make it successful, and then once that is successful, they start to branch out into other opportunities and do it all over again.

So, what is the secret behind having or Building a Successful Team?

Setting aside personal motivation for the greater good of the group so that one day it will be the funding source to support what you really want to do.

Let me write that again:

The secret behind Building a Successful Team is setting aside personal motivation for the greater good of the group so that one day it will be the funding source to support what you really want to do.

The old corporate America/retail acronym really holds true and definitely applies here—TEAM: together everyone achieves more—and as simple a statement as it is, with action it is extremely powerful. Together everyone achieves more.

For example, let's say…

- You want to start a shoe store.
- Bob wants to own a gas station.
- John wants to own a pet store.
- Susan wants to open a bowling alley.
- Mary wants to open a storage facility.

These are great business ideas and can be very profitable, but here is the problem: All five of you work jobs that consist of a forty-hour work week, don't have any funds or strong enough credit to get a business loan, and have absolutely no idea where to even start. So what happens? You learn what you can for the shoe store when you can; Bob learns what he can for the gas station; John, the pet store; Susan, the bowling alley; and Mary, the storage facility; but after five years, all five of you still work the same jobs, and none has made any real headway in actually opening a business other than maybe a sale here or there. You all talk amongst yourselves about your desires to open a business and be successful, but each one of you is only thinking of doing your own thing for yourself rather than coming together to figure out a way that you can all be successful and eventually all have the business that you desire. This is yet another example of a Rat Race that leads to absolutely nowhere. Some of you can relate, I'm sure.

Now, what's even worse is when you are fortunate enough to actually start the company or business and you have the same exact problem because you either have no idea what you are doing or you don't have any help and you're on your own. Does that sound familiar?

Next, to make things even worse, you also have those who have been to school for business but still have absolutely no idea what they are doing. And why is that? It's simple: because knowledge is absolutely useless if it is not utilized and exercised with action. Here is the secret: Knowing how to do something and never doing it is irrelevant. It is hard to take people who know how to fish but have never actually done it and make them equal to those who fish seven days a week, rain or shine, in order to feed their families and pay the bills. Action reigns supreme over knowing how any day in my book. I don't care if you're a straight-A student of fishing and have all the degrees and are up to speed on all the technology; if I am hungry and I am ready to invest my money for some fresh fish, I am putting my money with the one who does it every day and has a track record. This is a weird analogy, and I am actually starting to want fish, but nevertheless, the point still stands.

Don't get me wrong, I am not knocking school and education, because for some it is definitely needed, but I will tell you that not everyone is built for schooling, and for those of you out there, you know exactly what I am talking about. My ADD and OCD groups definitely know what I am talking about; some of the smartest people in the world were the worst students, and it has nothing to do with how smart they are but rather that they are very easily bored and annoyed—but that's another story.

Now, stop for a moment and let me clarify one thing: I do have a problem with someone going to school or college for two to four or eight years or however long and investing time and money into a certain field and then either not doing anything concerning that particular field afterwards or still being as dumb as the first day he or she started. I apologize, but this, in my opinion, is just a colossal waste of time, energy, and money, just an all-around bad investment. It amazes me how many people go to college for two or four years and yet still know absolutely nothing about their fields.

Sadly, there are many people who go to school just to trick themselves into believing that they are actually doing something productive with their lives or for the chump-change money left over from grants and programs that they could have easily earned by investing this same mostly wasted time into building their work ethic.

Excuse me for the brief tangent...

Bottom line, birds of a feather flock together, and studies show that people have the tendency to mimic the behavior of the five people they spend the most time with; this may be an extreme positive, or it could be an absolute nightmare.

If you are unhappy and want more out of life, then I encourage you to take a look around you and begin to evaluate your Circle of Influence, which would be the five people you spend the most time around.

Ask yourself, do they have the lifestyle that you are currently seeking to obtain for you and your family?

Is your Circle of Influence currently a beneficial and productive factor in your positive growth and development?

Are any of the behaviors and actions of the five people you spend the most time with a detriment and deterrent to your Personal Definition of Perfection?

You will not speak hundreds and thousands and receive millions and billions; you will not visualize tents and sleeping bags and receive a mansion; you will not imagine ten-speed mountain bikes and receive luxury cars; you will not think the minimum and receive the maximum results!

You must invest your time with like-minded individuals who are eagerly seeking to move forward to consistently and continuously improve their lives.

Surround yourself with those who encourage you, push you forward, have no problem with holding you accountable, and expect the same from you.

Understand that success comes in all different shapes and sizes and is a personal preference; a million may be successful for one individual and ten thousand may be successful for another, so there are no right or wrong numbers or any set standards in regard to achievements and accomplishments, and that is the intriguing beauty of it all.

Only you will know whether you are in a place of success, as it is solely up to you to determine what success means for you and then set your goals accordingly.

Who am I—who is anyone else, for that matter—to tell you that success equals a million dollars? Frankly, that is just not realistic and is another form of living by someone else's definitions instead of your own.

For example, if someone had an average balance of $30 in his or her bank account for the last five years and then was somehow able to acquire $100k in a six-month time frame, then this person may consider this to be success; however, if another person had an average balance of $75k for the last five years and now has a balance of $100k in a six-month time frame, although this is a $25k increase in the balance, this person may not consider this to be success.

Everyone is different and has his or her own personal definitions! There are several mentors and authors who recommend a healthy balance in your life, meaning there should be those people on a level below you whom you can help, there should be those who are equivalent, and then there should be those who are way ahead of you in life so you continue to learn, grow, and develop.

Building a Successful Team is the equivalent of building a successful life, and the quicker you realize this, the easier it will be for you to ultimately succeed.

Maximize the Secret Behind the Secret!

ACCOUNTABILITY SUMMARY:

The Accountability Summaries for Chapters 1–5 should be completed.

How to Build a Successful Team:

There are three supporting factors for success, and every wealthy or successful individual has one of these three things:

1. A mentor or coach
2. A team of people who want to achieve a certain goal
3. Systems

Needless to say, the very smart and very successful person usually has all three of these:

1. A mentor or coach
2. A team of people who want to achieve a certain goal
3. Systems

So basically, we can relate being wealthy and successful with having a mentor or coach, a team, and systems.

Upon completion of the Accountability Summary for Chapter 5, you were instructed to review your PERCS and align your thinking, visualizing, speaking, and actions to support what you desire for yourself and your family.

Once you have become comfortable and fully conquered this task, the next step is to unite and to actively seek out like-minded individuals who are seriously and sincerely interested in achieving the same goals as you so that you are not alone when it comes to holding yourself accountable for reaching, obtaining, and surpassing your goals.

Remember, birds of a feather flock together, and Building a Successful Team is no different—a bird is not a part of your flock if it does not possess the same feathers.

Notes:

Chapter 7
The Secret Behind the Secret

Congratulations to those of you who have invested your time to go through each chapter and have earned your way to the Final Destination.

I understand that this is a lot of information to take in, but I also know that there are those very rare few of you who actually get it.

At this point, you should really know, or at the very least have a pretty good idea, whether or not the information in this book resonates with you—whether you are willing to invest in yourself and take your current situation to the next level and whether you're ready to start living the life you want to live by your own definitions.

So, let's begin to review what we have covered in the previous six chapters:

1. We began with you providing yourself with an honest and realistic Personal Definition of Perfection.
2. We implemented a Desired Destination to assist you with Living by Your Own Definitions and being true to yourself rather than letting others define you.
3. You learned to utilize your Personal Definition of Perfection to Stop Running the Rat Race.
4. You maximized the Power of the Three-Letter Word with PERCS.
5. You changed the way you think with the Mindset of the Wealthy.

6. Finally, you learned to unite with like-minded individuals to assist with Building a Successful Team.

Now, here is what you have all been waiting for—it's time to reveal what truly is the Secret Behind the Secret, and hopefully you weren't waiting for some beautiful, sexy, overcomplicated answer.

If you have not figured it out by now, the Real Secret Behind the Secret of True Success is…

There is no secret!

Let me write that again:

The Real Secret Behind the Secret of True Success is, there is no secret!

There is just *you*!

Stop for a moment and let me help you right now.

You are your very best friend, and you are your own worst enemy!

Now imagine this as I write it again—really see yourself and let it resonate with you:

1. You are your very best friend.

Why? Because there is no one in this world and of this world who will ever know you better or treat you better than you can yourself. You know your desires, your likes, your truths, your ambitions, your goals, your wants, your needs, and everything else better than anybody else ever will. It is physically, emotionally, rationally, and humanly impossible to expect someone else to do more for you than you can do for yourself, yet we let marketing, advertising, what is popular and what is in style, the newest fashions and trends, dictate who we are and define us. Stop and think about it. Does that make good sense? Is that a winning scenario for you? You are your very best friend.

2. You are your own worst enemy.

Why? For the same exact reasons working in the reverse of your honest and realistic definitions of perfection, which are all due solely to the very choices that you have made in the past and present that ultimately dictate your future. Every hurt, every frustration, every feeling of inadequacy, and any other negative emotion that you carry is solely because of the choices you make, and because you know yourself better than anybody, you are the most dangerous person to have around you. Now let me clarify: I am not referring to the *action* (for example, someone else's actions toward you), because of course there are some things that happen in our lives by action that we do not control; however, no matter what action has taken place, we still have a choice as far as what to do or not to do because of the action. You can choose whether to hold on to that action or let it go, and that in itself is extremely powerful. The most powerful tool that you have in your possession is the power of choice, and it's the very choices you make that make you or break you by either building you up or tearing you down.

You truly are your very best friend, and you are your own worst enemy—it all begins with you, and it will all end with you.

So, begin right now by making a choice to be the very best friend to yourself that you can be by allowing yourself to live your life by your own Personal Definitions of Perfection and stop letting the world's system define you. You are the Secret Behind the Secret that ultimately decides whether you make it or break it in your life.

These are the principles I wish I had understood several years ago; with all sincerity, I know that I would have spared myself a lot of trials, tribulations, costly mistakes, and down-market moments and saved myself a lot of money in the process.

Nevertheless, I don't take any of it for granted, because the knowledge learned mixed with continuous and persistent actions is irreplaceable and priceless.

Imagine becoming a better person or building a better business and ultimately obtaining your Personal Definition of Perfection, whatever that means to you, whether it be earning more income, spending more time with your family and loved ones, taking your mind back from the system, or simply being happier and feeling more involved with your truths.

You must learn to Stop Running the Rat Race and begin to make choices to live your own life without following the crowd.

Unfortunately, a lot of unscrupulous individuals would take this opportunity to attempt to force you in one direction or the other, using fear to make you feel as if you're missing out on something if you don't do it this or that certain way.

I myself do not condone or support any tactics that promote fear, and that includes the fear of missing out.

Why? Because I don't need to tell you that whether it is today, tomorrow, or next year, if you don't take the necessary action, you are already missing out—you already know that.

I refuse to use babbling brainwashing tactics to make you feel like you need to do something that you already know in your heart you need to do.

- Are you tired of Running the Rat Race?
- Are you tired of playing the hamster on the same spinning wheel?
- Are you truly ready to stop being a follower and doing what everyone else is doing around you?

- Are you sick of being treated like a puppet on a string by the masses?
- Are you ready to find out who you really are and begin to define yourself by your own definition of perfection?
- Are you hungry to take yourself and/or your business to the next level?

If you are truly interested in succeeding and utilizing a proven system that actually works, then right now is your opportunity to make a true difference in your life.

- You are your best friend.
- You are your own worst enemy.
- Your life begins with you.
- Your life ends with you.
- You are the key to your success.

What is the Real Secret Behind the Secret of True Success?

There is *no secret*; there is just you, you, and more of you!

ACCOUNTABILITY SUMMARY:

The Accountability Summaries for Chapters 1–6 should be completed.

How to Maximize the Secret Behind the Secret:

- Know who you are.
- Know who you belong to.
- Know who you believe in.
- Know what you believe in.
- Know your truths.
- Know your strengths.
- Know your power.
- Know your rights.
- Know your desires.
- Know your goals.

True success is *always* accompanied by three major factors that *must* take place:

- Challenge
- Change
- Sacrifice

Why? Because there is no true success and accomplishment without…

- Overcoming challenges
- Making important changes
- A personal sacrifice

With growth and development come maturity and wisdom, as we are hopefully always evolving to the next positive thing; with this comes new revelation, which may bring about new Personal Definitions of Perfection.

What this means for you is that because the changes are inevitable, you will need to hold yourself accountable more than just once and periodically review and update your feedback notated within the Accountability Summary provided at the end of each chapter.

Needless to state, there is no better investment than that of you investing in yourself.

I sincerely trust that you will find your true value and continue to increase it as you begin Living by Your Own Definitions.

Notes:

Appendix

Now that you know the Real Secret Behind the Secret of True Success and have been provided specific tools to hold yourself accountable, what are you willing to do to live the life you desire?

Are you ready to make the changes and accept the challenges and sacrifices to make what you feel you deserve a reality?

You must be clear and understand exactly what your personal definitions are to take the necessary action.

There is no such thing as a get-rich-quick formula to succeeding, and fairy tales, magic potions, genies in a lamp, and wishful thinking are not going to produce long-term results.

You must make the choice to open up your mind to all the possibilities, get pumped up and motivated, and begin applying yourself and putting in the work.

Mentality and mindset are such crucial and pertinent factors to your growth and development.

Failure, fear, and lack are no longer an option for you or your family!

You must do your part if you plan to live in a state of More Than Enough!

"Opportunities are for those who dare to Play the Game and Rewards are for those who are determined to Win the Game."

Bonus Chapter
More Than Enough

How can a person live in a state of More Than Enough? Well, let's start by defining what More Than Enough is.

I want you to really think about it—what is the common denominator that ultimately defines living in a state of More Than Enough?

What is the one thing that will bring about the fulfillment of whatever desire you have that ultimately defines More Than Enough for you personally?

If you want more time with family or alone, more cars in the garage or driveway, more homes in different states or around the world, more clothes and shoes, more vacations and getaways to travel the world, or if you want to give more, do more, and contribute more to others, what exactly do you need to fulfill these desires?

I'm sure at this point, everyone knows that the simple answer is *money*, *money*, and *money*! You need money to accomplish every one of these criteria! At the end of the day, *money answereth all things*! There are no ifs, ands, or buts in that statement!

So, what am I stating exactly? Every issue, challenge, problem, altercation, struggle, pain, inconvenience, and any other negative criterion you can think of or that can hinder you in life—they ALL can be eliminated and managed by *money*!

I don't care how emotionally, physically, or mentally you want to take the scenario. At the end of it all is one answer: MONEY!

Studies show that the leading cause for divorce, murder, theft, suicide, and many other negative outcomes is money or, should I say, the lack thereof!

So why are we writing about More Than Enough? Well, there are several reasons right there that make it a pertinent topic to address, don't you think?

Are you currently happy with your life right now? Are you content living the way you live right now?

Are you OK with what you see around you, what your family, kids, parents, dogs, cats, neighbors, friends, associates, and co-workers see? Are you OK with your life right now, or can you honestly say that you want, need, and desire way more than you have right now?

I want you to think back to when you were younger and had those hopes and dreams to be such-and-such and to have such-and-such and to accomplish such-and-such; my question to you now is, do you actually have any of it? Was it all daydreams of wishing upon a star, or do you actually have any of the things that you dreamed as a kid to have and to accomplish?

If so, then great, but if not, why? And let me help you out here: Please don't be like the majority and start making all types of excuses for your personal failures and lack instead of manning or womanning up and taking responsibility for your actions. You and *only* you are the reason that you are exactly where you are right now, today, in your life!

This world that we live in (which I consider and like to call the *trap*) has provided you with so many distractions and excuses that it's almost numbing, things like living check to check, entertaining bad and negative debts, having little to no money in the bank or liquidity, lacking funds for the future, and the list goes on and on; however, they will promote the very things that will keep you in this state of mind by way of marketing and advertising things to you so that you feel compelled to be a part of something, and this is the systematic approach to keeping you *broke, broke, and more broke!*

There is a reason that they do not teach finances, credit education, debt management, budgeting, earning, and saving in grade school: Listen, the dumber you are with finances, the more money they make, point-blank and simple! They have no intention to educate you to be better in the very areas that put more and more money in their pockets, and why would they if exactly what they are doing to hustle you works day in and day out?

Sadly, the majority of people absolutely do not want to know, nor do they care about, the truth; they care only about exactly what has been brainwashed into them about what reality is and how things should be, which is exactly why the agenda is rampant and in full force. They know that 95 percent of the world is nothing more than a bunch of rats on their wheels and puppets on their strings, which makes 95 percent of people a condoning factor in the cause and zero threat. Really think about that!

You must go above and beyond to make sure you are increasing on a daily basis, enabling you to conquer the trap of life that has been set up for you; please don't be so naïve as to think that the world is here to support you and that they will have your back in your time of need; you will be so sadly mistaken, as your destruction spiritually, mentally, physically, emotionally, and financially is a clear part of the agenda.

I, Brian P. Lucas, am boldly stating, *no more! Those days end today, right here and right now!*

The Real Secret Behind the Secret of True Success

How will you ever have more than you have right now if you continue doing the same thing you have been doing all your life?

Remember, true success requires challenge, change, and sacrifice, and there is no way around it, regardless of how you attempt to go about it; you will ultimately have to give to get, and you will have to make it a priority to actually do something, because if there is no work then there is no eat! Simple!

It amazes me how everyone wants to be rich and talks this rich game, yet their mouths have more hours on them than every other part of their body. News flash: If you want, you'd best get up off your shoulders and your heels and go do something that coincides with the desires of your heart. Talk is cheap, and excuses are talk's best friend!

People who talk a lot but don't do a lot don't have a lot and are broke a lot!

A lazy person will never have the desires of his or her heart, and I don't care how you slice it and dice it, it just will never happen. I say that with all confidence—take that to the bank, cash it, and stash it!

Keep in mind, short-lived, or should I say fake and phony, success is not true success—it's hokey-pokey, rub a magic lamp with a genie and make three wishes. I know a lot of you buy into this fictitious fairy-tale way of living, but it will lead to destruction!

You know, sometimes you have to go into detail about what something is *not* to get to the simple answer of what something truly *is*, and that is exactly what you are experiencing right now; a lot of answers are already present, but sometimes it's the act of communication that brings what is buried deep inside you to the surface.

Too many times, people are sitting around with their hands out, waiting on someone else to do something for them, when they need to get up and get out and get to work and actually make strides to do something for themselves; this socialistic, dependent-on-everyone-else, and waiting-to-be-helped-by-the-more-fortunate attitude is yet another example of a trap!

Only losers sit around thinking that they actually deserve the same thing as someone else who worked harder and more efficiently; only those who have a piss-poor mentality and a broke person's mindset could really believe that a person who sits around doing nothing should be able to live in the luxuries of those who actually make a point to get out there and get it by any means necessary.

I apologize in advance, but I have zero pity for a person who doesn't work yet feels entitled to the same treatment and outcome as those who do. I have zero respect for a lazy, time-wasting, want-something-for-nothing person; socialism is for the weak at heart and the weak of mind.

Please understand that there are even teenagers making significant amounts of income by simply taking advantage of opportunities provided by today's technology, so please help me understand what the excuse is for the rest of the world!

So how will we learn to understand living in a state of More Than Enough?

Great question! Here is your answer: by simply eliminating anything and everything that is a contributing factor to living a life of Not Enough! If you are successfully able to eliminate the Not Enough, then you automatically increase your chances to live in a state of More Than Enough.

The definition of More Than Enough can be summed up for the purpose of this chapter as having more than enough money, so how exactly can we stop not having enough money?

By making a conscious effort to not waste what little we have, as every penny is a precious stepping stone that leads to More Than Enough! Every penny is another step forward!

Stop letting the world dictate who you are and who you are going to be by brainwashing you to think and act exactly the way they have pre-planned.

I understand a lot of this will go over the heads of 50 percent of the people who read this. Nevertheless, the point still remains: If you have to read this a hundred times before you actually get it, then I would advise you to do just that.

You will never be at peace until you understand that you are nothing more to the leaders of this world than a number on a piece of paper (hint, hint: your social security number) and no one in this world and of this world cares about you or your wellbeing or that of your family!

The very world you will die for will kill you without a second thought, and that is exactly what they are doing daily by way of suggestions, thoughts, and ideas that have you resembling the namesakes of one of the most-watched shows in America: *The Walking Dead*! Some would say, "What a coincidence!" However, I say it is exactly what it is, because I don't believe in coincidence. It's unfortunate—the majority of the world is exactly that, the walking dead, eyes wide shut; they don't have eyes to see or ears to hear!

All they know is what has been shoved down their throats by society through Hollywood movies, fake reality TV, music videos, cartoons, and the only-show-you-what-they-want-you-to-see news. What a joke!

More Than Enough

So, how many people are thinking to themselves right now, "I thought this chapter was about More Than Enough"?

Let me let you in on a little secret: You will *never* have More Than Enough until you admit to residing in the dungeon of Not Enough. Have you ever heard that you have to know where you are to know how to get to where you are trying to go?

Well, this holds true with living in a state of More Than Enough as well—it is not exempt from these basic principles.

Ask yourself these two simple questions right now: Does this information resonate with me? Do I see room for improvement in myself, my way of thinking, or how I currently live my life?

This is the start of being able to draft a map that locates the right now and then summarizes the steps you must take to get to where you are trying to go to live in a state of More Than Enough.

It is ultimately *you* and the way *you* think that bring about the change or more of the same!

I can assure you that if you think small, you will forever remain small, and you will never enter the Promised Land of More Than Enough; the words *small* and *More Than Enough* shouldn't even be in the same sentence or thought, as they contradict each other!

Those of you who think small will reap small rewards—you only get out what you put in!

You can't have a thousand-dollar mentality and be a multi-millionaire—it's *impossible*!

You can't have a Huffy or Mongoose let's-pedal-it-out mindset and drive a Bentley—it's *impossible*!

The bottom line is, you cannot have a loser attitude and be a winner—it's *impossible*!

The only thing a loser will win at is losing again and again, which only equals more and more loss!

One thing I have noticed is that a lot of people are always talking about all these things they want to do, what they want to accomplish, how they want to live, the home they want to live in, the vehicle they want to drive, all the destinations they want to travel to, all the clothes, shoes, purses, jewelry, etc. they want to have, but here is the major problem: They almost never have a game plan, a map to reach the destination, or an idea of how any of it will ever come to fruition; therefore, they are easily carried back and forth with the wind because they know only what they can physically see and what they are repeatedly told.

Ask yourself, why are so many people *broke* and living in a state of Not Enough?

Do you really think that people who are sane and in their right minds get up and choose to live their lives in poverty on a daily basis?

I guess I will go without eating today… I'm looking forward to making little to no money today… I think staying in a home that is falling apart is so cool… I love to push my car to the side of the road when it breaks down in the middle of traffic… Living a life of Not Enough is great!

Do you really think that anybody thinks or feels this way? Of course not!

So again, why are so many people broke and living in a state of Not Enough?

Well, because they don't know that there are realistic options that apply to them that can bring about a change. And why don't they know? Because there is no one there to guide them to a better life.

Sometimes, all people know is all people know. We are a product of our environment; whether we want to believe it or not, it's true! Now, do you have to be? No! But regardless, it's still true, because most of us are.

So, here is the question: What exactly are you prepared to do about it? What sacrifices are you willing to make so you no longer have to live in a state of Not Enough? How important is a change to you in your life right now?

What challenges, obstacles, and problems are you willing to overcome to break away from living in a state of Not Enough?

Not Enough is a mentality and a mindset birthed by the way you allow yourself to think!

Living in a state of More Than Enough is a mentality and a mindset birthed by the way you think!

Are you willing to make the changes in your way of thinking necessary to succeed?

Have you ever heard the expression "You are what you eat"? What exactly do you think this means?

As a person thinketh in his or her heart and mind, so is that person; you are exactly what you think you are, and you will have exactly what you think you will have!

So how strong is your thought process when it comes to you and who you believe you are?

You will *never* be more than you think yourself capable of! What do you see?

When you think about yourself, what comes to mind?

Are you a conqueror, an overcomer, a winner? Or are you easily defeated, afraid of change, and more of a loser? Now, what are you going to do about it?

How are you going to turn the tides with your thoughts about yourself and enable yourself to become all the things your heart desires?

Are you not tired of contributing to the negatives in your life? Is it not time for you to build a more positive attitude about yourself so you can take your life to the next level and begin to build a platform that allows the More Than Enough to begin performing on the stage of your life?

Seriously, you have to find it deep within yourself to finally ignore all the negatives that have been implanted in your life by others, the things people have said to discourage you and to make you feel as if you're inadequate, all the slick negative remarks from those who were hating and discrediting your dreams; you have to get rid of all that negativity and begin to build your own destiny that is in line with what you really believe and think about yourself in the light of accomplishment.

Stop giving your power and control over to others who do not have your best interests in mind and only want to use you, take advantage of you, manipulate you, and ultimately destroy you and all your dreams and desires for the future.

I can assure you that if you put all your eggs in someone else's basket (someone who does not cherish you or hold you in high regard), you will return empty and void with zero accomplishments and zero gain.

You cannot depend on others to come through and make things happen for you when you already know that you need to be up and out making moves for yourself. Do not put your destiny in someone else's hands—it's a big mistake that you will *never* live down because you cannot get that time back: once it is spent, it's gone forever, never to return.

Not Enough is not an option from this day forward, so you now have to make a conscious effort to manipulate a system that was put here to manipulate you so you can gain the control that is needed to push forward toward the prize of living in a state of More Than Enough!

You have to believe that it is doable and that the opportunity rightfully belongs to you too!

I don't care if you make only $25,000 a year—it is absolutely possible for you to make $100,000 a year if you make a point to adjust the way you think going forward.

The number does not matter—the only thing that matters is the mentality and the mindset; it can be $100,000 now; what is stopping you from making $500,000 or even $1 million?

Keep in mind, More Than Enough is More Than Enough, and everybody has a different definition for what that actually means to him or her personally.

More Than Enough will not necessarily mean being a millionaire for everyone, and this is perfectly OK. Simply find out what the definition of More Than Enough is for you and then plan accordingly to obtain, achieve, and exceed this goal until you're satisfied.

The bottom line is, if you think broke, you will forever be broke, and if you wait for More Than Enough to just show up with no hard work, then you will forever be broke. More Than Enough is readily available for all, but you have to actually *do* something to *get* something. Plant seeds and watch the harvest grow; if no seeds are planted, then no harvest grows. Simple!

Please understand it is absolutely possible to obtain continuous growth with the right mentality and mindset—you can take yourself from a place of Not Enough and put yourself on the road to More Than Enough with a clear vision and a map with the right directions.

If you are tired of living just to get by and you want more than a check-to-check life, then I strongly advise you to start working on your thinking and to attain your personal definition of More Than Enough!

You have to learn how to take massive action to receive great results. There are no magic pills, handouts, or get-rich-quick schemes that will provide you a life of More Than Enough.

ACCOUNTABILITY SUMMARY:

What ultimately defines More Than Enough for you right now?

Right now, I want you to dig deep within yourself and begin to define what your personal definition of More Than Enough is for you, your family, your children, and your sphere of influence.

Would it be to have $10,000 of liquidity in the bank? Would it be $20,000, $50,000, or only $5,000?

What do you personally consider to be More Than Enough for you right now?

We did a survey earlier this year asking one simple question:

If you had all the money you needed and you no longer had to work, what exactly would you do every day?

This is a very important exercise that allows you to locate yourself and come to the level of appreciation for what it is you actually would love to do day in and day out.

If you're somewhat hung up on what you feel you should be doing with your life, then this is a clear indicator and a great way to pull out of you what you really want in life.

Again, if you had all the money you needed and you no longer had to work, what exactly would you do every day?

Believe it or not, the number-one answer was travel, so let's use it as an example:

In your current state right now, are you able to pick up and travel whenever you want, go where you want, how you want, and stay as long as you want, with finances not being a determining factor or even a second thought?

I am asking you these questions purposely—I want you to grasp the concepts of living in a state of More Than Enough, and it all starts with the way you think: It is a mentality and a mindset.

Really ask yourself the aforementioned question and see what you come up with, because it sheds a bright light on what is really important to you and what you really would like to be doing all day.

Another question to ask yourself to bring about some awareness:

What is it that you like to do every day that makes you happy, is effortless, and makes time go by, something you would do all day for *free*, you love it so much?

Last but not least, you can simply get a piece of paper and pen and, on one side of the paper, write down the things you want to do and like to do, and then on the other, write down the things you have experience or expertise in.

Simply look for the common denominator or the most related answers on your paper, then go back to your prior answers from the previous questions and do the same thing; look for the common denominator for all your answers, and this will tell you what criteria you need to prepare for going forward.

Again, you will have to know exactly where you are before you can attempt to start going anywhere.

There will be challenges, changes, sacrifices, uncomfortable moments, what seem to be inconveniences, slight struggles, and hurdles to get over and come through, but remember, there is nothing that comes your way that is more than you can handle or more than you can bear; there is no such thing as coincidence, and if it came your way, then it was meant to be, and the victory belongs to you with each and every scenario that presents itself in your path to More Than Enough.

This is why it is so important to incorporate experience and exposure into your everyday schedule: so you are receiving an organized and structured representation of bigger and better things.

Imagine pulling up to a five-star resort in the car of your dreams, but before you get to the valet as you're pulling up, you see what seems to be a shiny presentation at a car lot, with all the cars you have ever dreamed of owning since childhood lined up in a row staring at you; this experience will no doubt excite you and stir something inside of you because you are being exposed to better and greater by personally striving to be the greatest person that you can be with your time here on earth.

If you really want to know what the service level of More Than Enough is, I would strongly advise that you and your family spend one full day at a five-star resort, and I can safely say that you will be amazed and so will they; experience service like never before from the time you pull onto the resort's grounds till the time you are ready to pull off into the sunset.

You have to be exposed to uncomfortable situations to experience the level of life that is foreign to you, and I can assure you that it will be worthwhile, because it will provide a mental picture that ultimately assists you with changing the way you view the world and the way you think.

Show me your thoughts, and I will show you your future actions, and with some basic studies of the way the world usually rotates, we will be able to determine the roundabout results of those very actions.

Whatever is important to you, you will consistently and continually think about it day in and day out, so you must search within yourself:

- What do you usually think about and meditate on throughout the day?
- Do these thoughts align with living in a state of More Than Enough?
- Do you honestly foresee yourself moving in a positive direction to obtain More Than Enough?
- Does the title More Than Enough know your name or even know who you are?
- What challenges, changes, and sacrifices are you willing to expose yourself to in order to obtain More Than Enough?

More Than Enough is more than just a revival or revolution; it's best described as a lifestyle!

So ask yourself, does this lifestyle resonate with you and the goals you want to achieve?

Be the best you that you can be and make it a priority to live in a state of More Than Enough right now.

Notes:

Notes:

The Conclusion

Who would have guessed that it was the real you that you were searching for all this time?

Once you know who you really are and make the choice to walk in your own shoes, you will begin to see major changes take place in your life.

This is not just some book to read that you say "amen" to and agree with that sits on some shelf collecting dust while you mimic the average person's life with no action, progress, or results.

People seriously need to stop believing in these fairy tales with magic beans, wishing upon stars, and rubbing lamps and waiting for a genie to pop out. This unearned self-entitlement creates a mindset of dependency and simultaneously builds a mentality that has the tendency to make a person believe that the world actually owes him or her something. Needless to state, this is the trap of all traps!

People who are OK with settling for handouts and freebies and barely getting by will never be a threat to the powers that be and will continue the cycle of lack in their families and in their Circles of Influence.

Remember, birds of a feather flock together, so if you don't like the feathers you see, then find some different birds to flock with. Simple!

Take a really hard look in the mirror and honestly see if you are pleased and satisfied with the reflection that you currently see; if there is any room for growth, development, or improvement, then this book may forever be a guide to help you reach that next monumental step in your life.

I sincerely hope that I have made the message abundantly clear for all those of you who are reading: It is not the book that makes the difference, but it is ultimately you who make the decision to change you. This book will not become another one of the personal crutches used to justify failure or lack. Do not expect change to come dropping out of the sky like rain just because you read it if there is no plan of action and personal accountability on your part.

The bottom line is, people do what is important to them; if change is important, then you will make the necessary adjustments to live the life you want to live in truth, rather than living the life the world has marketed and advertised you to live, which is a lie.

You must know who you are to be who you are, and you are your very best friend and your own worst enemy, all wrapped up in one beautiful package. It amazes me that most people will invest more time and energy into the very things they do not want rather than investing that same time and energy into the desires of their hearts.

Now is your time to break free of all the rules, regulations, traditions, and family curses and begin to walk in your greatness!

You are the equivalent of what you think and speak about yourself, and you will manifest what you think and what you speak; your life is a direct reflection of your level of faith.

Wisdom is the principal thing, and as you continuously seek wisdom, you will find all your truths.

Sincerely and respectfully,

Brian P. Lucas

BRIAN P. LUCAS

About the Author

Most importantly, above anything and everything else, I believe in and I trust the God in Heaven, which is the God of the Bible. I am a Christian, and I believe in God the Father, Jesus the Christ, and the Holy Spirit. I believe that Jesus is the Son of God and that Jesus died on the cross for my sins, transgressions, and unrighteousness. I believe in the resurrection that Jesus was raised from the dead and that Jesus now sits on the right hand of God the Father with all power in Heaven and on Earth. I respectfully believe without compromise, doubts, or any second thoughts that Jesus is the one and only way to God the Father and that Jesus is the one and only way to receive Salvation and Forgiveness by the Mercy and Grace of God.

Now, am I an angel, holier than thou, full of righteousness by my own power, religious, or perfect? No!

Frankly, if I were or if anyone else actually could be, then there would be no need for Jesus or a Savior, because we would just press our holiness button and save ourselves.

People may think to themselves, why would I write this information in the About the Author section, as this could hinder the sales, likes, or respect for the book itself? Here is my bold yet respectful response to those who may think so shallowly: I am *nothing* without God, and this book is *nothing* without me. Without me, this book does not exist, but without God, I do not exist; therefore, this book and everything else I possess belong to God anyway.

I Live by My Own Definitions, and I refuse to compromise on my faith and beliefs.

What is a person searching to find in the experiences of another?

Are you searching for signs and wonders with accolades, accomplishments, and trophies that are only self-promoting and self-indulging, that parade a person's greatness and excellence to justify his or her worth and value, to determine whether or not the person is credible enough to write a book or speak into your life?

I refuse to comply! I am equivalent to you, nothing more and nothing less; we are all one and the same.

One great thing about truth is that it is always true; whether it's coming from a doctor or a janitor, a multi-millionaire or someone living in poverty, someone driving a luxury car or someone riding a bicycle, a dope dealer on the corner or a preacher behind the pulpit, the truth is always the truth!

Truth in word will always resonate with those who are seeking it. My birds will know my feathers and flock with me, and the sheep I am responsible for will know my voice; I will resonate with them, and they will resonate with me.

I am but a lonely voice in the wilderness that has experienced my own personal road to Damascus and has been awakened to a glimpse of the truth that every human being is searching for.

I am just an everyday average person who one day realized that my destiny did not have to mimic those around me, and that I am special because there is only one me, and you are just as special because there is only one you.

I am that I am, not what the world tells me or attempts to market and advertise me to be. I came to a point in my life where I realized that I'm not a victim but was just very good at playing one.

My life forever changed when I came to the simple conclusion that the world owes me nothing and that I am not entitled to anything outside of my faith that I have not worked for or willed my way.

I now comprehend the importance of having eyes to see and ears to hear, which enables me to see through the deception the world is consistently promoting to the walking blind who have their eyes wide shut.

I strongly believe that ethics, morals, and character still mean something today, no matter what the way of this new world is shoving down our throat!

I promote unity over division, I support equality over slavery, and I respect hard work but not the lazy.

Mentality and mindset are key; stand for something, or you will fall for anything!

Here is my bio summed up:

I once was lost, but now I am found; I once was blind, but now I see.

My only goal and purpose in life is to open up the eyes of as many people as possible while I am still here, so that each day I am hopefully putting a smile on God's face.

Every day I want to imagine God saying, "Well done, good and faithful servant."

I am that I am because of who Jesus is.

I have what I have because of what Jesus has.

I can do what I do because of what Jesus did for me on the cross.

I am *nothing* without Jesus!

Every experience and accomplishment I am blessed to possess and all my joy come from the aforementioned.

Sincerely and respectfully,

Brian P. Lucas

BRIAN P. LUCAS

Author: Brian P. Lucas

Each and every day, seeds are being planted, and it is up to us to determine exactly how each seed will take root and manifest in our personal lives. The Harvest is dictated by the ground in which the seed is planted, and if the ground is good, then the Harvest has the potential to be great. We must empower the Good Ground in our lives in order to produce a Great Harvest for our families and future generations to come.

Pastor/Author: Henry L. Babers, Sr.

There are more people in this world today who don't know where they are in life than ever before. Some of them are very powerful, rich, and famous. This book provides the reader with answers from the word of God that will reshape their lives in a Christ-like manner. When we discover just how much God loves us and how he desires to bless us, it's exciting.

www.ingramcontent.com/pod-product-compliance
Lightning Source LLC
Chambersburg PA
CBHW072219070526
44585CB00015B/1400